Where Is
Michigan?

Where Is Michigan?

by Jennifer Marino Walters

illustrated by Ted Hammond

Penguin Workshop

To Pato: Thank you for introducing me
to your beautiful state!—JMW

PENGUIN WORKSHOP
An imprint of Penguin Random House LLC
1745 Broadway, New York, NY 10019
penguinrandomhouse.com

Designed and Produced by Dinardo Design, LLC.

Library of Congress Cataloging-in-Publication Data is available.

First published in the United States of America by Penguin Workshop, 2026

Manufactured in the United States of America
CJKW

ISBN 9798217053285 (paperback)
10 9 8 7 6 5 4 3 2 1

ISBN 9798217053292 (library binding)
10 9 8 7 6 5 4 3 2 1

The authorized representative in the EU for product safety and compliance is
Penguin Random House Ireland, Morrison Chambers, 32 Nassau Street,
Dublin D02 YH68, Ireland, https://eu-contact.penguin.ie.

Contents

Where Is Michigan?

Whether it's going to work, school, or the mall, cars are the main way Americans get from place to place. Over 90 percent of US households own at least one car.

When cars were first sold in the United States in the late 1890s, the average American couldn't even dream of owning one. Cars were expensive, and only very wealthy people could afford them. They also broke down frequently and got a lot of flat tires!

Henry Ford wanted to change that. He started the Ford Motor Company in Detroit, Michigan, in 1903 with the goal of making cars more affordable for everyone.

In 1908, Ford's company launched the Model T. It sold for about $850, about $20,000 in today's money. That made it affordable for more people, but still out of reach for many. Ford needed to find a way to lower the price even more.

In 1913, he found the answer. He began using a moving assembly line in his factory. A moving assembly line is a moving belt that carries a product along a line while people at stations add a specific part to it, or perform a specific task on it. Instead of one car being built by one person or team, now it could be built by many people who each did one specific job on the fast-moving line. The assembly line reduced the time it took to build a car from twelve hours to a little over one and a half hours. By 1925, the price of a Model T had dropped to under $300.

Once most people could own a Model T, life changed dramatically in America. People could travel around the country. Paved roads and highways were developed. Suburbs grew outside cities. And as more auto companies sprang up in Detroit and other Michigan cities, thousands of people moved to the state to work in them. Today, Detroit remains a major center of the US auto industry.

CHAPTER 1
Michigan's Land and Environment

Michigan is in the upper Midwest region of the United States. It is the tenth-largest state by population and the eleventh-largest by area. Michigan is sometimes called the Great Lakes State because it shares borders with four of the five Great Lakes—Lake Erie (say: EAR-ee), Lake Huron (say: HYUR-on), Lake Michigan, and Lake Superior (only Lake Ontario does not border Michigan). Because of this, Michigan has the longest freshwater coastline in the world at over 3,200 miles!

Michigan is bordered by Indiana, Ohio, and Wisconsin in the south, and by the Great Lakes and the country of Canada in the east, north, and west. The name "Michigan" comes from a word from the Ojibwe (say: oh-JIB-way) Nation that loosely translates to "big lake."

Over 40 percent of Michigan is covered in water. That makes it the state with the highest percentage of water coverage. Not all of Michigan's water is the Great Lakes. The state also has about eleven thousand inland lakes, over three hundred waterfalls, and hundreds of rivers.

Michigan is also one of the most heavily forested states—over half of it is covered in forestland. These forests are full of trees such as spruce, pine, oak, hickory, and maple.

Michigan stands out in another way: It's the only state that's split into two! Both land masses are peninsulas (land that's surrounded by water on three sides). They are called the Upper Peninsula and the Lower Peninsula. The Lower Peninsula is much larger than the Upper Peninsula.

More than 80 percent of Michigan's Upper Peninsula is forest. Though it's the size of

Connecticut, Delaware, Massachusetts, and Rhode Island combined, only a little over three hundred thousand people live in the Upper Peninsula. That's only 3 percent of Michigan's total population! Upper Peninsula (U.P.) residents are sometimes called "Yoopers," short for "U.P.ers."

The western part of the Upper Peninsula is home to several mountain ranges, including Michigan's highest point, the 1,979-foot Mount Arvon. The Porcupine Mountains—named by early adventurers who thought the outline of the trees resembled a porcupine's quills—are part of one of the oldest mountain chains in the world. They're about two billion years old! Porcupine Mountains Wilderness State Park includes some of Michigan's most beautiful scenery, including lush forest, cascading waterfalls, Lake Superior shoreline, and miles of rivers and streams.

Michigan's Lower Peninsula is mostly flat

and shaped like a mitten. Most Michiganders (the name for people who live in Michigan) live in the Lower Peninsula, which makes up nearly two-thirds of the state's land area. The Lower Peninsula has many beautiful beaches. These include Sleeping Bear Dunes National Lakeshore, with sand dunes as high as four hundred feet. Michigan's most populous city, Detroit (population over six hundred thousand) is in the Lower Peninsula. So is Michigan's capital, Lansing.

The Upper Peninsula and Lower Peninsula are connected by the Mackinac Bridge, also known as "Mighty Mac." At five miles long, it's one of the longest suspension bridges (bridges with a roadway supported by cables) in North America. It stretches across the Straits of Mackinac, a waterway that connects Lake Michigan on the west and Lake Huron in the east. In very strong winds, the bridge's center section moves! When that happens, the bridge temporarily closes so no cars can go across.

Michigan has 420 named islands in the Great Lakes. Some of them are popular vacation spots. Mackinac Island, located in Lake Huron between the Upper and Lower Peninsulas, is one of Michigan's most popular tourist attractions.

There are no vehicles allowed on the island—visitors can only get to it by ferry, boat, or plane. People get around Mackinac Island by walking, biking, or riding in horse-drawn carriages. They enjoy museums and historic buildings, outdoor activities, dining, and shopping.

Isle Royale, part of a national park in Lake Superior, is only accessible by boat or seaplane. Because of its remote location, it's one of the least visited US national parks. Visitors can go camping, hike through forests, and stroll along rugged shorelines.

The Great Lakes have been popular transportation routes for many years, and their waters are home to roughly six thousand shipwrecks. About 1,500 of them are in Michigan's waters. At the Michigan Underwater Preserves, scuba divers can explore over two hundred of these shipwrecks, but they can't take anything—it's against the law.

A Floating Post Office

The Detroit River in Michigan is home to America's only floating post office! The forty-five-foot *J.W. Westcott II* tugboat began operating as an official United States Postal Service mail boat in 1948. It delivers mail to passing ships on the river. The *Westcott* has the world's first non-military floating zip code, 48222.

From early April to late December, the *Westcott* is open twenty-four hours a day, seven days a week. It gives the thousands of sailors who spend months at a time on the river a connection to home. In addition to letters, *Westcott* crew members deliver everything from toiletries to food to TVs. For more than thirty years, a woman named Arlene Earl delivered flowers to captains and crew members on the ships via the *Westcott*. One time, the *Westcott* even helped to deliver a goat to a petting farm!

How does the *Westcott* deliver the mail? First, it drives alongside the ship at the same speed. Then, mail carriers use a system of ropes and buckets to get the mail onto the ship.

Michigan's lush forests are home to a variety of animals, such as bears, deer, rabbits, elk, and moose. The state also has more than 450 species of birds, including water birds like great blue herons and piping plovers, raptors such as ospreys and peregrine falcons, and the rare Kirtland's warbler. Michigan reptiles include red-bellied snakes

and spiny soft-shell turtles, while green frogs, bullfrogs, and marbled salamanders are some of the state's amphibians.

Despite its nickname as the Wolverine State, very few wolverines still live in Michigan. In fact, the last wolverine sighting was in 2004! So how did the nickname "Wolverine State" come about?

Experts don't agree, but some believe it came from Michigan's history as a fur-trading center, where fur traders from places like Canada may have sold wolverine pelts.

Michigan has a continental climate. That means the temperature changes throughout the seasons. The southern and central parts of the Lower Peninsula have hot summers and cold winters. The northern part of the Lower Peninsula and the entire Upper Peninsula have shorter summers and longer, colder winters. Michigan averages thirty to forty inches of precipitation yearly, but some parts of the Upper Peninsula and the northern Lower Peninsula get almost 160 inches of snow per year!

CHAPTER 2
State Origins

The first people to live in the area now known as Michigan are believed to have arrived as early as twelve thousand years ago. They were called the Anishinaabe (say: ah-nish-in-AH-bay) people, and they spoke Algonquian (say: al-GON-kwee-in) languages. The largest nations of the Anishinaabe included the Ottawa, the Ojibwe, and the Potawatomi (say: pah-tah-WAH-tuh-mee). These three nations formed an alliance (a union in which groups work together) known as the Council of Three Fires. They lived in villages of dome-shaped houses called wigwams.

Most of the early inhabitants of Michigan lived near lakes and traveled by water. The Anishinaabe lived in villages in the summer where they farmed corn, beans, and squash, and gathered berries, seeds, and nuts. In winter they moved in order to hunt deer, elk, beaver, and other animals. They also fished, traded, and traveled the waters in canoes made of birch bark.

All of these people—as well as smaller numbers of Huron peoples, who spoke an Iroquoian (say: ear-uh-KWOY-en) language—were living in what is now Michigan when the first European set foot there in 1622. He was a French-born Canadian explorer named Étienne Brulé (say: eh-TEE-en BROO-lay).

Other French groups soon followed and began settling in the area. There was fighting between the French and the Indigenous peoples at first, but they soon developed relationships with one another. Many Indigenous men became fur trappers and traded with the French settlers. Sometimes Indigenous women would cook food to sell to the French. The settlers brought diseases

from Europe that were devastating to Indigenous communities, as well as guns and alcohol.

In 1668, Frenchman Pere Jacques Marquette founded the oldest European settlement in present-day Michigan, Sault Sainte Marie (say: SOO saint muh-REE), in the northeastern part of what is today the Upper Peninsula. The French set up a Roman Catholic mission (a place to teach or do the work of the church) there. Other missions soon followed. Some Indigenous people lived and studied at them.

In 1701, French explorer and army officer Antoine de la Mothe Cadillac (say: AN-twon day la moth CAD-ill-ack) founded Fort Pontchartrain (say: PONT-sher-train) du Detroit (now Detroit) in the southeastern part of present-day Michigan as a center for fur trading. France offered free land to entice French people to move to Detroit.

By the mid-1700s, France controlled large parts of what is now eastern Canada, most of the Great Lakes region, and the land west of the Appalachian Mountains (including present-day Michigan). Britain controlled the thirteen colonies that later became the United States, which lie along the East Coast. Both countries wanted control of the upper Ohio River Valley. That area included what is now northeastern Ohio and western Pennsylvania. This led to the French and Indian War (1754–1763).

Because of their trade agreements, some Indigenous nations fought on the side of the French or the British. The British won and gained control of Canada and most of the French territory east of the Mississippi River, including present-day Michigan. The British did not develop good relationships with the Indigenous people living in present-day Michigan. They put strict limits on the amount of goods Indigenous people could trade, and they moved further into Indigenous lands. In response, Indigenous forces began to attack British forts, and the British fought back.

In 1763, Ottawa leader Pontiac led an attack on Detroit called Pontiac's Siege. The siege lasted for more than four months. The British held out, and the Indigenous forces eventually surrendered. The area remained under British control.

Detroit served as an important British supply center during the American Revolution from 1775 to 1783. Still, they couldn't win the war. The colonies won independence from Great Britain and formed the United States. The Treaty of Paris awarded present-day Michigan to the United States in 1783.

Over the next several decades, the United States began taking over Indigenous lands. The US government forced Indigenous nations to sign unfair treaties to avoid violence. In the 1821 Treaty of Chicago, the Potawatomi, Ojibwe, and Ottawa peoples had to give up roughly four million acres of land in present-day Michigan. Some of them moved to areas west of the Mississippi River. Others fled to Canada or resettled on reservations (areas of land set aside for Indigenous people to live on, often far from their own homes) in Michigan. In 1830, President Andrew Jackson passed the Indian Removal Act. The act forced Indigenous peoples to leave their homes east of the Mississippi River—including in Michigan— and move to areas west of the Mississippi (mainly in present-day Kansas and Oklahoma).

A second Treaty of Chicago in 1833 forced the Potawatomi, Ojibwe, and Ottawa to give up their remaining reservations in Michigan. Some refused to leave, and the United States government sent the US Army to violently remove them from their lands. Only a small number of Ojibwe and Potawatomi remained in Michigan.

As Indigenous peoples were forced out of Michigan, more settlers came from other states.

The Erie Canal, completed in 1825, connected
the Great Lakes to the Hudson River and New
York City. Many people from New York and
the New England states moved to Michigan via
the canal. They worked as farmers, merchants,
shipbuilders, and lumbermen.

A huge wave of immigration to Michigan in the 1830s became known as "Michigan fever." Michigan's population grew quickly, from 29,000 in 1830 to 212,000 by 1840. Many of Michigan's early settlers were of European descent. Large numbers of Germans settled in Detroit. The

Dutch settled in the western part of the area, while Finnish, Irish, and Cornish people worked as copper miners in the Upper Peninsula. They helped to develop new mining techniques and technologies. Copper mining also led to the opening of mining schools, like the Michigan Mining School (now Michigan Technological University), to train engineers to operate copper mines. Many Polish people also moved to Michigan.

In 1835, Michigan approved a constitution and formed a state government. But it couldn't become a US state until it ended a dispute with Ohio over a narrow piece of land called the Toledo Strip. Congress eventually awarded the land to Ohio, while Michigan received the western part of the Upper Peninsula. Michigan officially became a US state in 1837. It was a free state, meaning it did not allow slavery.

Mining and forestry became very important

parts of Michigan's economy. Many French Canadian immigrants settled in Michigan during the late 1800s and early 1900s. From around 1870 until the end of the nineteenth century, Michigan led the United States in lumber production. By the turn of the century, Michigan's economy would transform again.

CHAPTER 3
Growth, Development, and Industry

Michigan grew with the invention of the automobile industry. Ransom E. Olds, who spent his childhood in Lansing working on all types of engines, founded the Olds Motor Vehicle Company in 1897.

In 1899, Henry Ford, born on his family's farm near Dearborn, Michigan, helped start the Detroit Automobile Company. His partners there grew impatient with his focus on improving rather than selling cars. He eventually left the Detroit Automobile Company and started the Ford Motor Company in 1903. He wanted to build a car that ordinary people could enjoy, not just wealthy people. He set a goal of producing one thousand cars per day.

In 1908, the Ford Motor Company introduced the Model T. Ford moved the company to a large factory in Highland Park (a city on the outskirts of Detroit) in 1910. About the size of forty-five football fields, the factory had so many glass windows it became known as the Crystal Palace.

After Ford introduced the moving assembly line in 1913, the cost of producing the Model T went way down, and the company was able to lower the price. That made the Model T the first car that was widely accessible to many more Americans. Millions of people began driving cars, making people living on farms less isolated. Cars became important to the economy, leading to the construction of a highway system and the growth of suburbs as cities spread outward.

Michigan quickly became the hub of automobile production in America—especially Detroit. W.C. Durant of Flint had started the General Motors Company in 1908 as the Model

T was introduced, and Walter P. Chrysler founded the Chrysler Corporation in Detroit in 1925. Ford, General Motors, and Chrysler became known as the "Big Three" auto companies. Auto plants were also built in other Michigan cities, like Grand Rapids, Lansing, and Pontiac.

Detroit came to be known as the automobile capital of the world. The industry paid well, and thousands of people moved to Michigan from Europe and across the United States to work in it.

Detroit's Black population also grew rapidly in the early 1900s due to the Great Migration. From about 1920 to 1970, millions of Black people moved from the South to northern cities such as Philadelphia and New York to escape unfair treatment including segregation (the separation of Black people and white people in public places like schools, buses, and restrooms). The number of Black people in Detroit jumped from about 6,000 in 1910 to around 150,000 in 1930!

During World War II (1939–1945), Michigan shifted its manufacturing to meet the needs of the armed forces. Detroit's automobile makers, in particular, were responsible for producing thousands of military vehicles, including armored cars, fighter planes, and tanks.

After the war, Detroit continued to grow, and so did its Black population. Detroit became a hub of jazz and blues music. Musicians like Miles Davis and Charlie Parker played at clubs throughout the city. Then, Detroit native Berry Gordy Jr. introduced a new style of music to

the world. In 1959, he founded a record label called Tamla Records. Later, Gordy changed the name to Motown Records, a nod to Detroit's Motor City nickname. He bought a building in Detroit to house a recording studio and called it Hitsville U.S.A.

Gordy began signing mostly Black singers, musicians, songwriters, and producers from Detroit and around the United States to create a genre of music all its own—Motown. Motown is a type of soul music that blends gospel, pop, and rhythm and blues. During the 1960s and 1970s, Motown gained popularity as singers like Smokey Robinson (from Detroit), Stevie Wonder (from Saginaw, Michigan), and Diana Ross (from Detroit) cranked out hits.

In 1972, Berry moved Motown Records to Los Angeles. Hitsville U.S.A. eventually became the Motown Museum, which today is one of southeast Michigan's most popular tourist destinations. Detroit still has a strong music scene: It has made huge contributions to punk rock. It's also considered the birthplace of techno, a form of electronic dance music. Three Detroit teenagers—Juan Atkins, Kevin Saunderson, and Derrick May—created the new genre after spending hours listening to electronic music from overseas in the late 1970s and early 1980s. They became known as the Belleville Three, named for their school, Belleville High School.

CHAPTER 4
Today's State

Today, the Big Three automakers still have factories in the Detroit area (though Chrysler is now called Stellantis). Many other auto companies, including Dodge and Chevrolet (say: shev-ro-LAY), are also in Michigan. About 20 percent of the state's workforce (over one million people) work in the auto industry.

Though the number of farms in Michigan has been declining since the late 1900s, agriculture is still a big part of Michigan's economy. Only California produces a more diverse variety of crops, meat, and dairy products. Most Michigan farms are in the southern half of the Lower Peninsula. Some of the biggest crops are corn, wheat, soybeans, sugar beets, potatoes, and flowers.

Many fruits are also grown in Michigan, including cherries, apples, grapes, peaches, blueberries, pears, plums, and strawberries. The state is a big source of vegetables such as cucumbers, celery, asparagus, carrots, and pumpkins, too. And the dairy industry is important, with Michigan being one of the top producers of milk in the United States.

Mining still takes place in Michigan. The western part of the Upper Peninsula is a top producer of iron ore. Limestone (used to make concrete, mortar, and cement), gravel, and sand are also mined in Michigan. Rogers City, on the Lower Peninsula's northeast coast, is home to the largest limestone quarry (a place where large amounts of stone are dug out of the ground) in the world.

With so much natural beauty, history, and culture throughout Michigan, it's no surprise that tourism is another important part of the economy. Many tourist attractions showcase the heritage and culture of the various immigrants who helped shape the state.

At Nelis' Dutch Village in the city of Holland, located in the southwestern part of the state, dancers dressed in costumes of the Netherlands perform folk dances. Visitors can tour a giant

windmill from the Netherlands, make Dutch cookies, and carve wooden shoes. Holland also hosts the famous annual Tulip Time Festival, which features over six million tulips and has attracted millions of visitors throughout the years.

Colonial Michilimackinac (say: mish-ee-lee-MACK-in-aw) is a 1700s-era British fort and trading village on the shores of Lake Michigan.

Visitors can meet costumed guides dressed as British soldiers and French Canadian merchants and see eighteenth-century military demonstrations, food preparation, and gardening.

Frankenmuth is a German-inspired town in the east-central part of Michigan. Visitors can enjoy German food and drinks, horse-drawn carriage rides, festivals, a maze with thousands

of mirrors, an outdoor adventure park, and Bronner's Christmas Wonderland, the world's largest Christmas store.

At the Henry Ford Museum of American Innovation in Dearborn, visitors can see the oldest surviving American car and the Quadricycle— the first car built by Henry Ford. At neighboring Greenfield Village, visitors can ride in a real Model T or on a steam-powered locomotive!

Roughly a hundred thousand members of Indigenous nations still live in Michigan today, in both the Upper and Lower Peninsulas. Most are members of the Ojibwe, Ottawa, and Potawatomi Nations. These nations continue to share common customs, language, and beliefs.

Students from all over the United States and the world attend college in Michigan. The state's two largest universities, Michigan State University in East Lansing and the University of Michigan in Ann Arbor, are big rivals. Magic Johnson,

Students graduating from Keweenaw Bay
Ojibwe Community College

considered one of the National Basketball Association's greatest all-time players, was born in Lansing and played basketball for Michigan State. Michigan Stadium, where the University of Michigan's football team plays, is the largest football stadium in the Western Hemisphere. It can hold a whopping 107,601 fans!

The two universities are known for more than just their sports. Both Michigan State and the University of Michigan are considered major research institutions. The University of Michigan is the state's oldest college, founded in 1817. When Michigan State was founded in 1855, it was called the Agricultural College of the State of Michigan and was the first agricultural college in the United States. It still has a large agriculture program.

Student artists from around the world in grades 3–12 come to Interlochen in northwest Michigan to attend the prestigious—and highly competitive—Interlochen Arts Academy for boarding school or summer arts camp.

Professional sports are also big in Michigan. Major League Baseball's Detroit Tigers and the National Hockey League's Detroit Red Wings have dedicated fan bases. The Red Wings have won the Stanley Cup championship eleven times (more than any other US team), earning Detroit yet another nickname: "Hockeytown." The National Football League's Lions and the National Basketball Association's Pistons are also based in the Detroit metro area. NASCAR races take place at the Michigan International Speedway in Brooklyn.

From its rich cultural institutions to its breathtaking beauty, Michigan is truly a gem of the Midwest. It's no wonder that over 128 million tourists flock to the state each year!

Michigan at a Glance

Statehood: 1837

Nickname: The Wolverine State

Abbreviation: MI

State Motto: *Si quaeris peninsulam amoenam circumspice* (Latin for "If you seek a pleasant peninsula, look about you")

State Tree: Eastern white pine

State Animal: White-tailed deer

Capital: Lansing

Size: 96,713 square miles

Population: Over 10 million

Famous People from Michigan:

Madonna (singer), Floyd Mayweather Jr. (boxer), Larry Page (Google cofounder), Kristen Bell (actress, singer, and voice of Anna in *Frozen*)

★ Lansing

State flag

State flower
Apple blossom

State bird
American robin

FUN FACT:

The first three-color, four-way traffic light was installed in Detroit in 1920. It was invented by Detroit police officer William Potts, who added the yellow "caution" light to the existing red and green lights.

Timeline of Michigan

1622 — French explorer Étienne Brulé becomes the first European to visit what is now Michigan

1701 — French explorer Antoine de la Mothe Cadillac founds Fort Pontchartrain du Detroit, now Detroit

1763 — The British gain control of Michigan after the French and Indian War

1783 — The Treaty of Paris awards what is now Michigan to the United States

1817 — Michigan's first college, the University of Michigan, is established

1837 — Michigan becomes the twenty-sixth US state

1903 — Henry Ford founds the Ford Motor Company in Detroit

1913 — Ford starts using the moving assembly line, dramatically lowering the time it takes to make the Model T

1948 — The *J.W. Westcott II*, America's only floating post office, begins delivering mail to ships on the Detroit River

1959 — Berry Gordy Jr. founds Tamla Records in Detroit, later changing the name to Motown Records

2023 — The University of Michigan Wolverines win the Big Ten college football championship

Timeline of the World

1620	Pilgrims from England arrive in Plymouth, Massachusetts, aboard the *Mayflower*
1660	Charles II becomes king of England
1707	Japan's Mount Fuji erupts for the first time in ten thousand years
1752	Benjamin Franklin invents the lightning rod
1787	The US Constitution is signed
1818	Mary Shelley publishes *Frankenstein*
1844	Samuel Morse sends the world's first message via telegraph; it says, "What hath God wrought?"
1901	Walt Disney is born
1910	Earth passes through the tail of Halley's Comet
1914	World War I begins
1945	The United Nations is formed
1962	The Beatles release their first hit song, "Love Me Do"
1977	NASA's space shuttle *Enterprise* makes its first test flight
2024	Mexico elects its first female president, Claudia Sheinbaum

Bibliography

*Books for young readers

*Dunphy, Maureen. *All About the Great Lakes*. All About . . .
Places. Indianapolis: Blue River Press, 2020.

*Gregory, Josh. *My United States: Michigan*. A True Book. New
York: Scholastic Inc., 2017.

*Yasuda, Anita. *What's Great About Michigan?* Our Great States.
Minneapolis: Lerner Publishing Group, 2016.

Websites

Michigan History Center:
www.michigan.gov/mhc/michigan-history
Michiganology: www.michiganology.org
Pure Michigan: www.michigan.org